D0646989

This is no longer
the property of
King County Library System

FEB   2015

Cardinals

Wil Mara

Cavendish
Square

New York

Published in 2015 by Cavendish Square Publishing, LLC
243 5th Avenue, Suite 136, New York, NY 10016

Copyright © 2015 by Cavendish Square Publishing, LLC

First Edition

No part of this publication may be reproduced, stored in a retrieval system, or transmitted in any form or by any means—electronic, mechanical, photocopying, recording, or otherwise—without the prior permission of the copyright owner. Request for permission should be addressed to Permissions, Cavendish Square Publishing, 243 5th Avenue, Suite 136, New York, NY 10016. Tel (877) 980-4450; fax (877) 980-4454.

Website: cavendishsq.com

This publication represents the opinions and views of the author based on his or her personal experience, knowledge, and research. The information in this book serves as a general guide only. The author and publisher have used their best efforts in preparing this book and disclaim liability rising directly or indirectly from the use and application of this book.

CPSIA Compliance Information: Batch #WS14CSQ

All websites were available and accurate when this book was sent to press.

Library of Congress Cataloging-in-Publication Data

Mara, Wil.
Cardinals / Wil Mara.
pages cm. — (Backyard safari)
Includes index.
ISBN 978-1-62712-822-3 (hardcover) ISBN 978-1-62712-823-0 (paperback) ISBN 978-1-62712-824-7 (ebook)
1. Cardinals (Birds)—Juvenile literature. I. Title.

QL696.P2438M37 2014
598.8'83—dc23

2013047681

Editorial Director: Dean Miller
Editor: Andrew Coddington
Copy Editor: Cynthia Roby
Art Director: Jeffrey Talbot
Designer: Joseph Macri
Photo Researcher: J8 Media
Production Manager: Jennifer Ryder-Talbot
Production Editor: David McNamara

The photographs in this book are used by permission and through the courtesy of: Cover photo by Don Johnston/All Canada Photos/Getty Images; Johann Schumacher/Photolibrary/Getty Images, 4; H .H. Fox Photography/Flickr Open/Getty Images, 5; Bonnie Taylor Barry/Shutterstock.com, 6; © Jen St. Louis Photography/Flickr Open/Getty Images 8; D Trocio Photography/Flickr Open/Getty Images, 11; Tom Vezo/Minden Pictures/ Getty Images, 12; © iStockphoto.com/Angelafoto, 13; imagebroker.net/SuperStock, 17; © iStockphoto.com/Csaba Toth, 20; Larry Keller, Lititz Pa./ Flickr/Getty Images, 23; John Cancalosi/Photolibrary/Getty Images, 23; George Grall/National Geographic/Getty Images, 23; suebmtl/ Shutterstock.com, 23; Steve & Dave Maslowski/Photo Researchers/Getty Images, 24; Glenn Bartley/All Canada Photos/Getty Images, 26.

Printed in the United States of America

Contents

Introduction

Have you ever watched a squirrel chasing another squirrel around a tree, or a group of deer leaping gracefully through a stretch of winter woods? If you have, then you know how wonderful it is to discover nature for yourself. Each book in the Backyard Safari series takes you step-by-step on an easy outdoor adventure, and then helps you identify the animals you've found. You'll also learn ways to attract, observe, and protect these valuable creatures. As you read, be on the lookout for the Safari Tips and Trek Talk facts sprinkled throughout the book. Ready? The fun starts just steps from your back door!

ONE
A Cardinal's Life

There are many cardinal **species** throughout North America. The most common and geographically widespread among these birds is the northern cardinal, which bears the scientific name *Cardinalis cardinalis*. Most **ornithologists,** meaning people who study birds, consider the northern cardinal to be a medium-sized bird. Adult cardinals measure from seven to nine inches (18 to 23 centimeters) long and have a wingspan of ten to twelve inches (25 to 30 cm). Typical adult weight for the species is between 1.1 and 2.2 ounces (31 to 62 grams), with the males a bit heavier than the females.

Female cardinals usually only have a little of the vibrant red coloring that distinguishes the males.

Males differ from females in another, even more significant way: they possess the bright red coloration for which the northern cardinal is known. A typical adult male cardinal is red over most of its body, with some darker tinting along the wings and tail. It will also have a distinctive black "mask" that runs across the eyes and just below the beak. The beak is usually reddish-orange in color.

The female cardinal, however, has more of a grayish-brown coloring with some traces of red along the wings and tail feathers. The black mask common to males is not always present in the females, but each share the reddish-orange beak. Both males and females also share a crest, which is the small tuft of feathers on the top of their heads that, when extended upward, gives the head a pointy appearance.

This image shows the striking contrast between male and female coloration.

Trek Talk

Why are male cardinals so red? Believe it or not, it's primarily because of what they eat. Many of their favorite foods contain carotenoids, which are the naturally occurring colors found in many fruits and vegetables. Studies have shown that cardinals fed low amounts of carotenoids actually lose the brightness of their red pigmentation, meaning coloration, and become dull.

Where They Live

The northern cardinal is found in many parts of the United States, mostly in the eastern half. They also live farther south throughout Mexico as well as in parts of Guatemala and Belize. Many are found in southern Canada.

Other cardinal species and subspecies occur in the western half of the United States, as well as in parts of southern Canada and Mexico. Humans have introduced, or brought, northern cardinals into parts of California, Hawaii, and Bermuda. Although the birds were not native to these areas, they were able to successfully establish themselves, or settle down. This means that in these areas, northern cardinals are now considered an **introduced species**.

Northern cardinals can thrive in a wide variety of **habitats** from quiet, unpopulated woodland regions to crowded towns and cities. They are found near waterways, along the edges of heavily forested areas, in and around swamplands, and in the yards of homes and other buildings. They prefer plenty of cover, or shelter, and tend to build their nests in thick shrubs, dense hedgerows, and wild thickets. Yet they are not as secretive as you may think. They do show themselves frequently, so an attentive observer should have no trouble spotting them.

Cardinals can thrive in a variety of habitats, but their preference is wooded areas with plenty of coverage.

What They Do

The northern cardinal is generally a **diurnal** creature, which means it is active during daylight hours (as opposed to **nocturnal** animals, which are active during the night). You can expect to see cardinals at most any time during the day, but they are busiest in the early morning and the evening. They are quite territorial at times, which means they can be very protective of the general area in which they live. They are most territorial during breeding season, when they feel protective toward their mates as well as their young. The rest of the year, however, they are more relaxed. During the winter months they will even gather in a flock, or a large group. It is important to note that the northern cardinal is not a **migrating** bird, which means it does not fly off to reach warmer climates during the cold months. Instead, it will remain in its home **range** all year long.

Northern cardinals, like all birds and mammals, are homoeothermic, meaning warm blooded. As long as they can find decent sources of food throughout the winter season, their bodies can turn that food into energy, which creates heat. Northern cardinals cannot grow extra feathers to protect them from the cold, but they can "fluff up." Fluffing up not only creates a space of air between the northern cardinal's individual feathers, but also between its feathers and skin. This is like putting on a winter coat.

Most of the northern cardinal's diet is made up of grains, fruits, and vegetable matter. Their strong beaks allow them to crack open a variety of seeds, although they prefer those that are easily husked. Northern cardinals are also known to eat live food from time to time, including various bugs, worms, and creatures that grow and live in or near water, such as snails and clams. They are mostly ground feeders, which means they will land on the ground and hop around in search of things to eat. But they are not as picky during the winter months when food sources are not as abundant.

The Cycle of Life

The breeding cycle for cardinals usually begins in early spring. During this time the males will bring food to, and feed, the females. This "mate feeding" is a sign of pair bonding. Male cardinals will court and then mate with their chosen female. The two will then remain together for life. This includes the off-season, or the time when they are not breeding. Although the female is solely responsible for building the nest, the male will bring her much of the building material, including tough grasses, tree bark, and pliable twigs. Nest building usually takes between three and nine days to complete.

Female cardinals usually hatch two **broods** per year: one in early to mid spring and the other in late spring to midsummer. Each brood

A male cardinal courts a female with "mate feeding." These two will remain together for life.

normally hatches from three to four eggs, which have a pale whitish base color and are marked with medium to dark brown spatter. The male will provide food for the female while she is guarding and **incubating** the eggs, which will hatch in about two weeks. Baby northern cardinals, called hatchlings, are blind and without feathers. They quickly adopt the mother's grayish-brown coloring. The males will develop vivid red feathers as they grow into adults.

Both male and female adult cardinals will feed their young because hatchlings are helpless when born. The babies are fed live foods, such as insects, almost exclusively. After eight days, the young cardinals are nearly the size of the adults. In nine to ten days, they will be ready to leave the nest.

The oldest wild cardinal known to researchers lived at least fifteen years and nine months, but the average is much less. Because cardinals attract a great number of **predators**, many do not live through their first year.

A female cardinal will typically lay three to four eggs in a season, and both male and female will share the feeding duties.

TWO
You Are the Explorer

Bird watching is one of the most relaxing and rewarding outdoor activities. There are millions of people around the world who enjoy this pastime every day. Cardinals make particularly good study subjects because they are quite common, relatively comfortable around humans, and very beautiful. Once you understand the importance of giving them their space without disturbing them, you will begin to see the fascinating lives they lead.

What Do I Wear?

* Clothes that are loose-fitting and comfortable
* Old clothes that can get dirty
* Clothes that aren't too bright or vivid in color—remember, you don't want to disturb or frighten the cardinals
* A jacket, gloves, hat, and other warm clothing if you are going out during cold weather
* Any type of shoes will do, but those with soft soles will be the quietest. Also, if you have to do a lot of walking, you'll want to be comfortable. In the winter, you might need boots.
* Bug spray, particularly if you're going into forested areas near waterways during the warmer months

What Do I Take?

* Binoculars. A good pair of binoculars will be the most important piece of equipment you can bring along on your safari. It's important to remember that you should never try to get too

close to a cardinal, particularly during breeding season.

✳ A cell phone
✳ Folding chair or blanket
✳ Digital camera, particularly one that can retain good focus while zooming
✳ Notebook
✳ Pen or pencil
✳ A snack for yourself

Where Do I Go?

Cardinals can be found in a wide variety of habitats and are relatively comfortable around people. This is good news for you! No matter where you live—be it in the country, suburbs, or city—you should be able to find a few cardinals within a reasonable distance from your home. Remember that they spend the majority of their time off the ground, usually coming down only to search for seeds, fruits, vegetables, and occasionally insects. They may also swoop low to scare off predators that are invading their territory. But again, most of the cardinals you spot will likely be flying, or perched somewhere in a hedge or on a branch.

Safari Tip

If you are in an area where you know cardinals exist but you're having no luck getting them to come within a reasonable distance, try spreading some birdseed along the ground. If possible, use a mixture designed specifically for cardinals and other birds related to the species. Move away from the area where you dropped the seeds so that the birds feel comfortable coming down to feed. At the very least, you'll be able to observe them through your binoculars. You can also take some excellent pictures.

❋ Thick shrubs and other overgrowth. During breeding season—most of the spring and into part of the summer—cardinals will build their nests in wild places where they feel their young will be most protected. This will usually be shrubs and hedges, or any other area that has thick overgrowth.

❋ Wooded areas. Cardinals, like many other wild animals, prefer forested areas. They don't require the same degree of privacy and cover as some other birds except when caring for their young. At that time, their nests can be almost impossible to find. So try going close to waterways, such as streams or lakes, particularly areas with dense overgrowth.

✳ In and around farmlands. Cardinals know that they can always find a meal for themselves on a farm. Smart safari enthusiasts know that they will be able to find cardinals within that same area. This is one place where you will want to keep a close eye on your surroundings, as there will be many insects on a farm and a great deal of fallen fruits and berries.

✳ Your very own backyard. Do you have any hedgerows or wild thickets? Are there other homes in your surrounding area with bird feeders? Cardinals are perfectly happy to share their world with humans as long as they are left alone most of the time. During breeding season, it's not unusual to see a cardinal flying in and out of a hedge because there is likely a nest inside. Even outside the breeding season, they still spend much of their day searching for food. So don't dismiss the idea of looking for cardinals right outside your own window!

Trek Talk

Warning! Do not disturb cardinals when they are caring for their young. If you do see a cardinal flying to and from its nest, you are free to observe it—but don't get too close. They can become aggressive and even violent when agitated.

Whenever you plan a cardinal safari, make sure you have an adult you trust with you. It can be dangerous to walk around alone. Similarly, before you go on someone else's property, make sure you have permission to do so first. Travelling through property that isn't yours can get you into serious trouble. Farms, for example, are a great place to find cardinals, but you should never explore there if you are not allowed to.

What Do I Do?

✻ Be patient. This might be the most important safari tip of all. You may not spot a cardinal immediately. That's normal. Cardinals live in the wild all the time and are extremely cautious when they sense danger. This means they'll probably know you're there long before you know they are.

* Go out during the day. Remember that cardinals are diurnal creatures, so you shouldn't plan a night safari. The best time to locate cardinals is very early in the morning when they're fully rested and active. You can also go on your safari at sunset, when cardinals feel a bit safer from predators. Many will come out at that time and search for food.

* Listen. Cardinals are very musical, and this can help your safari tremendously. Try to go online and listen to sound samples of their songs and their calls. Many bird enthusiasts can identify bird **species** simply by the sounds they make. This is something you can learn how to do, too. Once you've memorized that distinct cardinal sound, you'll be amazed how much it will help you locate one in the wild. Many bird enthusiasts have located cardinals by hearing them well before actually seeing them.

* Don't make distracting noises or movements. Cardinals, like most other wild animals, will quickly become nervous in the company of humans. Once you've located a cardinal or two (or more), plant yourself in a good observation spot and stay there. Remain quiet and still. The cardinals will relax and go about their business, which is the point of your safari: to observe these birds in their natural environment.

✤ Keep your camera ready at all times. Pictures of cardinals make great souvenirs from your safari, but you need to be ready to take a picture when the opportunity presents itself. You may not have much time to snap a picture before a cardinal flies away, so try to keep your camera on and ready. You should also avoid using the flash if you can help it. The light from your camera could frighten the cardinals.

✤ Make notes. After you've observed a few cardinals, write down any information that you feel is important. What were they doing? Where were you when you saw them? What time of day was it? After you gather enough data, you'll begin to recognize patterns that'll help you with future safaris.

✤ When you return home, download any pictures (or videos, since most cameras take those as well) you took. Show them to your friends and family. You could also write a formal journal using both your pictures and your notes. Keep an ongoing record of your cardinal safaris from year to year.

THREE
A Guide to Cardinals

The most common and widespread cardinal is the northern species known as *Cardinalis cardinalis*. But there are other related groups and species within the family Cardinalidae found in North and Central America, such as tanagers and grosbeaks. Some are quite rare. Others are fairly numerous if you happen to live in the right areas.

Refer back to the notes you made while on your safari and consider the following questions:

* Is the bird predominantly red, with a distinctive black mask over its face?
* Were the tail and wing feathers a little darker than the bright red coloring of the chest?
* Were the eyes round and very dark, almost black?
* If not red, is the bird mostly a grayish-brown color, but with an orangish beak?
* Does the bird you wrote about above have some streaks of red (normally found on the males) along its wings and tail feathers?

* Does the bird possess the characteristic "pointy" tuft on the top of its head?

* Does the bird resemble a male in every way except its wings? Were its wings very black, contrasting sharply with the red coloring of the rest of its body?

* Was the bird a different color than described above? In that case, it could be a member of the Cardinalidae family, but not a *Cardinalis cardinalis.*

Now, look at the next page and see if any of the cardinals in the photos match the **characteristics** that you noted in your answers. Remember that you should use other information, such as your location (town, state, and country). Include the time of year during which you made your observations. This is particularly important if you live in the western half of the United States or in Central America, where many other Cardinalidae varieties are found. Try doing a little research on the Internet, too. Further resources are also provided for you in this book's "Find Out More" section.

Northern Cardinal

Desert Cardinal

Rose-breasted Grosbeak

Scarlet Tanager

FOUR

Try This!
Projects You Can Do

Cardinals are not suitable as pets, and you certainly can't go into the wild and live with them. But you can further your interest in cardinals in other hands-on ways when you're not busy on one of your safaris. Here are a few fun and easy projects that you can do along with your other cardinal activities.

Bird Feeders

Cardinals need food like every other living thing, and unlike some other birds, cardinals love eating from bird feeders. Food is hard enough for them to find on any given day, so they'll greatly appreciate any help you can give them.

What Do I Need?

* A bird feeder (can be purchased at your local home-improvement center or department store)
* Bird seed
* A tree in a quiet area of the yard

What Do I Do?

* Once you've acquired all your materials, choose a place to hang your bird feeder. If you have a nice, thick hedgerow on your property, hang the feeder as close to it as you can. The cardinals will feel safer using it if they don't have to wander too far from their homes or nests.
* After you've hung your feeder, stock it with birdseed. You can choose from a variety of birdseeds and other bird treats. There are even some blends made especially for cardinals and similar birds.

✿ Once your local cardinals discover the feeder, they will visit it quite often. Other birds, and even a few squirrels, will visit the feeder as well, so be sure to keep it well stocked. Once you start getting regular visitors, you'll be able to observe the birds from your window!

Opening the Lines of Communication

Cardinals make noises in order to communicate with each another, but there's no reason you can't try to get involved in the conversation!

What Do I Need?

✿ Your hands and voice

✿ A bush or tree to hide behind

What Do I Do?

✿ In order to "talk" with the cardinals, you will have to learn their various calls. You can search for hundreds of cardinal sound files on the Internet.

✿ Next, practice imitating these calls until they sound similar to the calls of actual birds. While they don't have to be exactly perfect, the closer you can get to mimicking a cardinal, the better.

❋ When you spot a cardinal on one of your next safaris, listen first to the sounds it's making, then try to make the same sound on your own. The real excitement will come when you draw the bird's attention to you. It may even call back!

Home Building

You could try to build a standard birdhouse for your local cardinals, but the truth is that they probably won't use it (and it would eventually be occupied by birds of some other species). However, you can do a little landscaping that might bring a few cardinals onto your property.

What Do I Need?

❋ A little land to spare that's not being used for much else

❋ A few inexpensive shrubs or hedges from your local garden center. These should be fairly dense because the cardinals will want to be covered. For your own enjoyment, try to purchase plant species that you find attractive and can add a nice touch of beauty to the landscape.

❋ A shovel

What Do I Do?

All that's left is to pick a place in your yard for your garden and plant your shrubs. Gardening in general is a pleasant pastime, so you'll probably enjoy planting and caring for whatever greenery you select. As soon as a few cardinals take up residence in your hedges, remember to keep your distance when observing them. Once they begin building nests and laying eggs, you know they've become comfortable in the home you've created for them.

Cardinal First Aid

You may encounter a cardinal that is sick or wounded during one of your safaris. Cardinals are known, for example, for crashing into reflective surfaces, such as house or car windows, when they are agitated. They mistake the reflected image for another bird. A wounded cardinal would be moving slowly, unable to fly, or lying on the ground. In an attempt to help, you may want to get close to it. Don't. First, you could frighten it so badly that it may die right on the spot. Birds are also known to carry diseases that can be very harmful to humans. If you have an adult with you (which you always should while on safari), ask that person to call your local animal control organization (most towns have them), zoo, or police department. If you see a cardinal that is suffering, be smart and let someone else take care of the situation. Do not try to handle it on your own.

Glossary

brood	a group of young birds that were hatched and cared for at the same time
characteristic	a specific trait or quality that an animal has, such as tan fur or brown eyes
diurnal	active during the day
habitat	the exact type of place in which an animal lives, such as a burrow, cave, or shoreline
incubating	keeping eggs warm so the embryos will develop properly; an embryo is the stage of the bird's development prior to hatching
introduced species	a species that did not previously live in a certain geographical area, but was then brought in to that area (usually by humans) and began to thrive
migrating	moving from one geographical location to another; many species of bird will move from one area to another at different times of the year
nocturnal	active during the night
ornithologist	a scientist who studies birds
predator	an animal that hunts other animals for food
range	the general area in which an animal lives
species	one particular type of animal

Find Out More

Books

Cate, Annette LeBlanc. *Look Up! Bird-watching In Your Own Backyard.* Somerville, MA: Candlewick Press, 2013.

Porter, Adele. *Wild About Northeastern Birds: A Youth's Guide.* Cambridge, MN: Adventure Publications, 2010.

Truit, Trudi Strain. *Birds.* New York, NY: Cavendish Square, 2011.

Websites

Cardinals / National Geographic

animals.nationalgeographic.com/animals/birds/cardinal

This website offers basic information about the American cardinal, along with beautiful illustrations, a range map, and audio files.

BioKids—Northern Cardinal

www.biokids.umich.edu/critters/Cardinalis_cardinalis/

Here you will find lots of basic facts and excellent photos of cardinals; links to other useful sites and good reference material can be found here as well.

Northern Cardinal / Cornell Lab of Ornithology ('All About Birds')

www.allaboutbirds.org/guide/northern_cardinal/id

Great overall information about cardinals and a terrific selection of easy-to-play cardinal sound files can be found on this website.

Index

Page numbers in **boldface** are illustrations.

About the Author

WIL MARA is the award-winning author of more than 140 books. He began his writing career with several titles about herpetology— the study of reptiles and amphibians. Since then he has branched out into other subject areas and continues to write educational books for children. To find out more about his work, you can visit his website at www.wilmara.com.